TABLE OF CONTENTS

HUMBLE POP STAR

Ed Sheeran is a British singer-songwriter. He is known for his bright-red mop of hair and his ability to tell stories through music. Ed writes songs about growing up, fame, love, and loss.

*Ed Sheeran has won many awards for his music, including four **Grammy Awards**.*

A Crabtree Branches Book

Today's Stars

ED SHEERAN

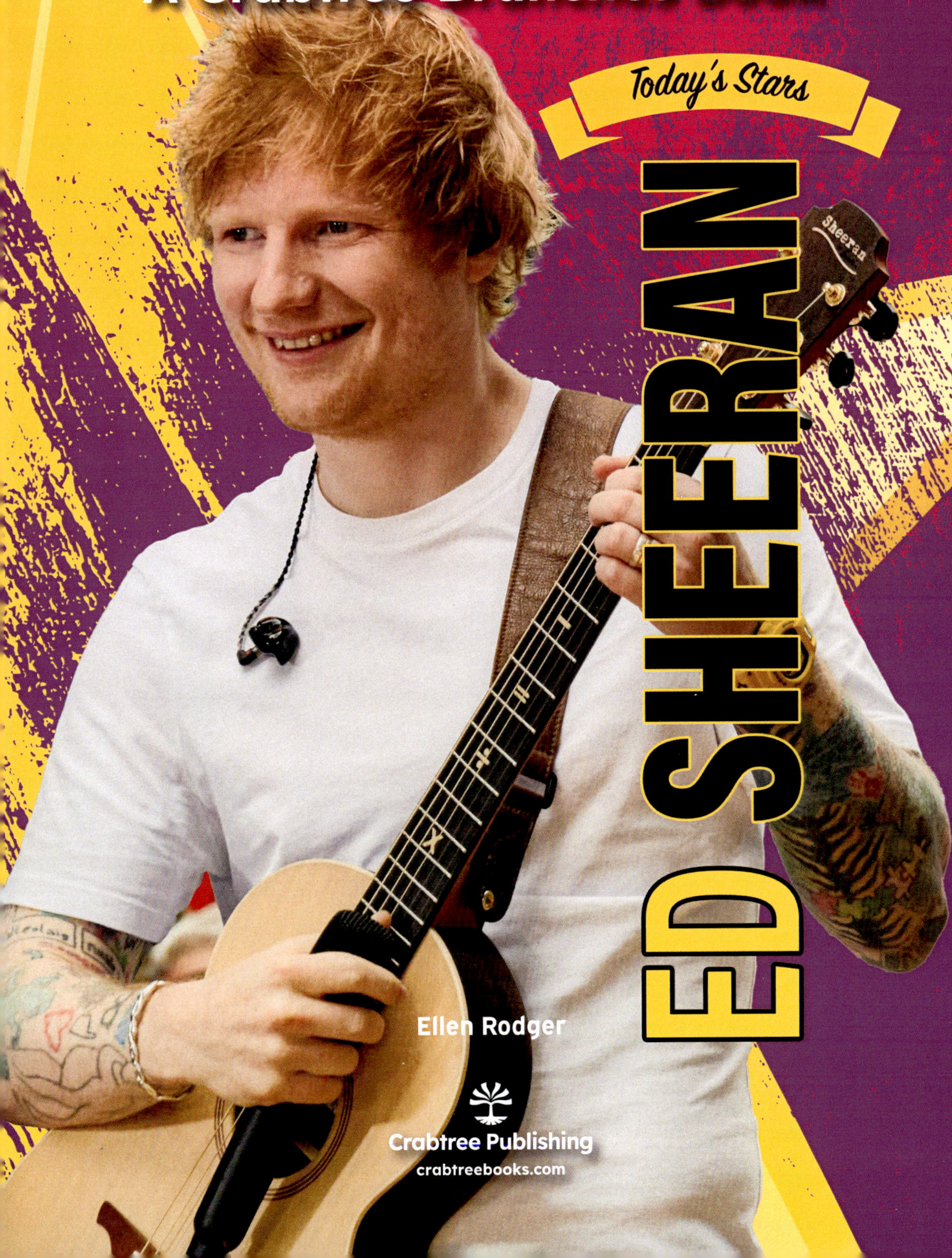

Ellen Rodger

Crabtree Publishing
crabtreebooks.com

School-to-Home Support for Caregivers and Teachers

This high-interest book is designed to motivate striving students with engaging topics while building fluency, vocabulary, and an interest in reading. Here are a few questions and activities to help the reader build upon his or her comprehension skills.

Before Reading:

- *What do I think this book is about?*
- *What do I know about this topic?*
- *What do I want to learn about this topic?*
- *Why am I reading this book?*

During Reading:

- *I wonder why...*
- *I'm curious to know...*
- *How is this like something I already know?*
- *What have I learned so far?*

After Reading:

- *What was the author trying to teach me?*
- *What are some details?*
- *How did the photographs and captions help me understand more?*
- *Read the book again and look for the vocabulary words.*
- *What questions do I still have?*

Extension Activities:

- *What was your favorite part of the book? Write a paragraph on it.*
- *Draw a picture of your favorite thing you learned from the book.*

Fun Facts

Ed released a number-one single on iTunes before even signing with a record label.

Fans of Ed Sheeran are known as "Sheerios." They love his **humble** nature and honest, friendly manner. Ed knows that his success comes from his ability to connect with people.

Ed is one of the world's best-selling music artists, with more than 150 million records sold worldwide.

Early on, Ed was inspired by many different musicians. These included The Beatles, Bob Dylan, Eric Clapton, and Irish singer Damien Rice.

The Beatles

Bob Dylan

Eric Clapton

Damien Rice

EARLY YEARS

Edward Christopher Sheeran was born on February 17, 1991, in Halifax, England. His parents, John and Imogen, raised Ed and his older brother Matthew in the small village of Framlingham.

Ed's parents encouraged an interest in music and art.

As a child, Ed wore thick glasses. He was born with just one eardrum. He also stuttered. At the age of four, Ed started singing in a church choir. He felt at home singing, and it helped his stuttering.

Singing can make it easier for a person who stutters to express themselves.

When Ed was nine, his uncle bought him the Eminem album *The Marshall Mathers*. Ed studied it hard. He improved his speech by learning all the lyrics.

Eminem

When he was 11, Ed met Irish musician Damien Rice at a concert. The meeting inspired him to become a musician.

Fun Facts

Ed's song "Castle on the Hill" was inspired by Framlingham Castle in his hometown. The video for the song features the castle, which was built in the 12th century.

MAKING MUSIC

Throughout school, Ed continued to work on his songwriting and guitar skills. By the time he was 11, he had his first **gig**. He performed an Eric Clapton song in front of his classmates!

At 13, Ed started recording and releasing his music. He then went to London at age 14 to **busk** and find gigs. Ed was determined to make a career in music.

Ed released his first EP, The Orange Room, *in 2005. An EP is a musical recording that contains fewer songs than an album.*

When he was 16, Ed was accepted into a music and theater school in London. It gave him the confidence to perform in front of crowds. Soon, he was a working musician.

Once Ed's music career started to take off in London, he became the opening act for more ***established*** *musicians.*

Fun Facts

At the beginning of his career, Ed made and sold his own recordings. He played hundreds of gigs, but was often homeless and slept on friends' couches.

LEAP INTO STARDOM

Ed was clever about building a life as a musician. He used social media to **promote** himself. He wanted to bring his work to an American audience. In 2010, Ed went to Los Angeles and dropped his music off at radio stations.

Los Angeles, California, is home to many major record labels and recording studios.

His music got noticed by actor, singer, and radio host Jamie Foxx. Jamie invited Ed to play at an **open mic** night. Ed wowed his first American crowd. This was just the beginning.

Jamie Foxx and Ed have remained close friends, with Jamie being one of Ed's biggest supporters.

Ed was soon writing and releasing several collections of music on his own. His first album, + (Plus), was released in 2011. Ed's songs began to soar on the music charts.

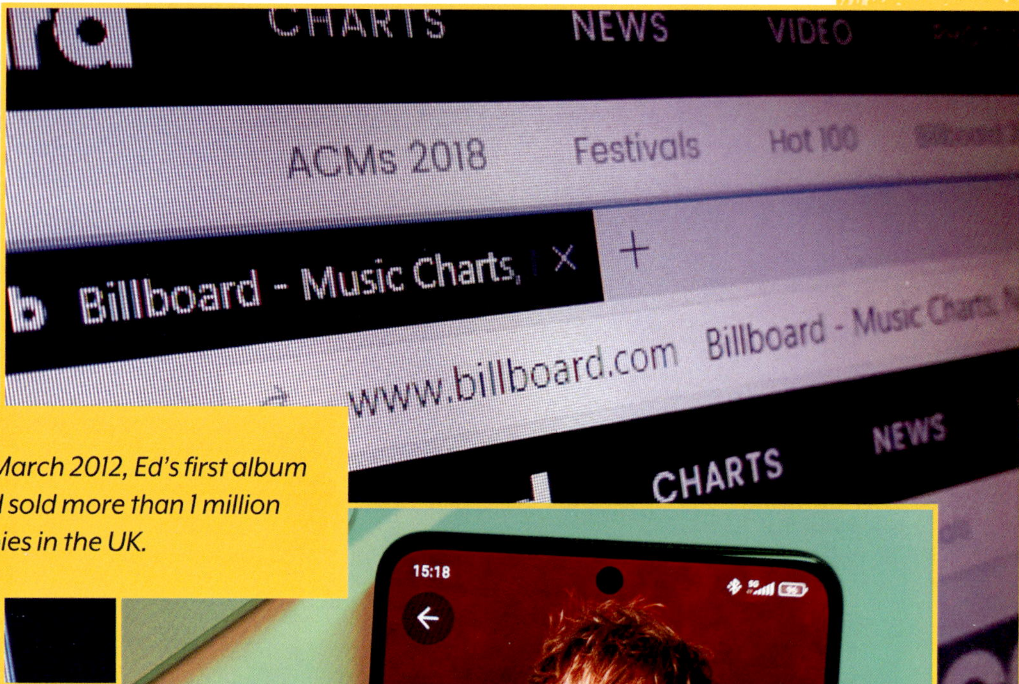

By March 2012, Ed's first album had sold more than 1 million copies in the UK.

Fun Facts

Ed loves tattoos. He has more than 60! When his first album reached number one in the UK, Ed had a plus symbol tattooed on his left wrist.

MUSICAL SUCCESS

Making music is all Ed has ever wanted to do. When his career took off, he was **elated** and grateful. Now he could buy a house instead of sleeping on someone's couch.

Ed bought his first home, a farmhouse in his hometown of Framlingham, in 2012.

Ed's music is different. He sings romantic **ballads** and pop songs with a twist of rap, R&B, and folk. But he makes it all work.

Ed's song "LEGO House" is about his favorite construction toy. It is also about building relationships.

Album success meant Ed started playing larger concerts. Instead of crowds of 20 to 200 people, he was playing to more than 100,000 people each night.

Ed's music has also earned him awards from all over the world, in many different musical categories. These include Grammy Awards for Song of the Year and Best Pop Vocal Album.

Ed has also won two MTV Video Music Awards (VMAs) and eight Billboard Music Awards.

DOWN TO EARTH

Ed is known for his casual style. This includes the way he dresses and how he connects with people. He's most comfortable in jeans, a T-shirt, and running shoes.

While Ed prefers a casual look, he "cleans up" well in tailored suits for formal occasions.

Fun Facts

In 2017, Ed was made a Member of the Order of the British Empire (MBE). This is a British honor that recognizes people who have made a great impact on others.

Giving back to others is important to Ed. He supports other artists by giving money to organizations that support young musicians. He also supports many charities, including hospitals and **hospices** for sick people.

Ed has performed at fundraisers, giving time and money. He's even donated items of clothing and guitars for charity auctions.

Fame and fortune have allowed Ed to purchase a small share in a British football, or soccer, club. In 2024, he became part owner of Ipswich Town Football Club in the Premier League.

Ed is a lifelong fan of Ipswich Town Football Club, which is located not far from his hometown of Framlingham.

Ed Sheeran is a down-to-Earth singer-songwriter. He loves what he does and works hard at it.

Ed names his guitars. He has several, and they include Felix, Lloyd, Cyril, and Nigel.

Ed doesn't think he is more talented than others. He believes his success was partly due to self-belief and **persistence**.

Ed has said that "Success happens from failing hundreds of times." He believes that only by failing over and over again was he able to learn what he was doing.

GLOSSARY

ballads (BAL-uhds): Light, simple songs, often about love

busk (buhsk): To entertain, often by singing or playing music, on the street or in a public place

elated (ih-LEY-tid): Being very happy or proud of something

established (ih-STAB-lisht): Being successful for a long period of time

gig (gig): A live performance by a musician or group

Grammy Awards (GRAM-ee uh-WAWRDS): Awards given by the Recording Academy of the United States to recognize outstanding achievements in music

hospice (HOS-pis): A place that provides care for people who are dying

humble (HUHM-buhl): To be modest, or not proud or arrogant

open mic (OH-puhn mahyk): An event during which anyone is welcome to sing or perform stand-up comedy, usually without auditioning first

persistence (per-SIS-tuhns): The quality that allows someone to keep going in spite of discouragement, obstacles, or opposition

promote (pruh-MOHT): To help or encourage something through advertising or another means

INDEX

WEBSITES TO VISIT

https://www.edsheeran.com

https://kids.kiddle.co/Ed_Sheeran

https://www.grammy.com/artists/ed-sheeran/6178

ABOUT THE AUTHOR

Ellen Rodger won a bank-sponsored short story contest at age nine. It was the last thing her bank ever gave her for free, but it kicked-started a career in newspaper, magazine, and book publishing. Ellen has written hundreds of books for curious young people, on topics as varied as the history of the potato, urban wildlife, refugees, the Great Lakes, and explorers.

Crabtree Publishing

crabtreebooks.com 800-387-7650

Written by: Ellen Rodger
Designed by: Kathy Walsh
Series Development: James Earley
Editor: Melissa Boyce
Educational Consultant: Marie Lemke M.Ed.
Production manager: Candice Campbell

Hardcover: 978-1-0398-8040-5
Paperback: 978-1-0398-8400-7
Ebook (pdf): 978-1-0398-8160-0
Epub: 978-1-0398-8280-5

Printed in the U.S.A./CP2025

Published in Canada
Crabtree Publishing
616 Welland Ave.
St. Catharines, Ontario
L2M 5V6

Published in the United States
Crabtree Publishing
347 Fifth Ave
Suite 1402-145
New York, NY 10016

Library and Archives Canada Cataloguing in Publication
Available at Library and Archives Canada

Library of Congress Cataloging-in-Publication Data
Available at the Library of Congress

Photographs
Alamy: Everett Collection Inc, p 8, PA Images, p 25, 26
Shutterstock: Paul Froggatt, cover, title page; Fred Duval, TOC, p 5; yakub88, p 4, p 24, p 28; Cineberg, p 6 (top), ; Brian Patterson Photos, p 6 (bottom); Elena_Alex_Ferns, p 7 (top left); landmarkmedia, p 7 (bottom left); Andrea Raffin, p 10 (bottom); Everett Collection, p 17; Stanislau Palaukou, p 18 (top) ; Rokas Tenys, p 18 (bottom); Paul Froggatt, p 19; Miguel Angel Lopez Rojas, p 20; Yulia Vasilyeva p 21 (top); Cloudy Design p 21 (bottom); Adam McCullough, p 22 (top); Bunsinth-Nan-Pua, p 22 (bottom) s_bukley, p 23 (left); Ga Fullner, p 23 (right); Rob Atherton, p 27; Mohammad Reza Yusmani, p 29 (top); Jasni, p 29 (bottom)
Wikimedia: Creative Commons, p 7 (top right), (bottom right), p 10 (top), p 11, p 15
All other images from Shutterstock